Vitaly Semeniuk

Study on the chemical composition of carbonated drinks

Vitaly Semeniuk

Study on the chemical composition of carbonated drinks

And their effects on the human body

ScienciaScripts

Imprint

Cover image: www.ingimage.com

This book is a translation from the original published under ISBN 978-613-9-88781-1.

Publisher:
Sciencia Scripts
is a trademark of
Dodo Books Indian Ocean Ltd., member of the OmniScriptum S.R.L Publishing group
str. A.Russo 15, of. 61, Chisinau-2068, Republic of Moldova Europe
Printed at: see last page
ISBN: 978-620-3-99759-0

Contents

INTRODUCTION

Abstract of the paper. This paper examines the negative impact of carbonated drinks on the human body. The information about the history of carbonated drinks, their composition, and their harm is examined. A questionnaire study of carbonated drinks and an experiment proving the negative effects of carbonated drinks are analysed. The composition of carbonated drinks is studied by means of an experimental label and chemical composition. The negative effects of carbonated drinks on the human body are promoted.

The relevance of the study lies in the current abuse of carbonated drinks by adolescents as a result of a lack of information about their harm to the body.

Purpose of the study: To examine the chemical composition of carbonated drinks and the effects of their components on the human body.

The following **tasks** are addressed in the course of the study:

1. Research information on the composition and properties of carbonated drinks on the internet and in popular science literature.
2. Conduct a questionnaire survey among students and offer advice on the consumption of carbonated drinks.
3. Study the composition of carbonated drinks on the label and conduct a comparative analysis of the samples of carbonated drinks under investigation.

Hypothesis: carbonated drinks may contain various substances that can have a negative impact on human health, disrupting the gut microflora, causing stomach problems and destroying dental enamel.

The object of the study is carbonated drinks from different manufacturers.

Subject: The ingredients of carbonated soft drinks and their impact on human health.

Research methods: theoretical analysis, questionnaire survey, experiment, quantitative processing of results, method of generalisation.

To answer the first question of what sparkling water is, we consulted Ozhegov's explanatory dictionary and learned that:

Carbonated beverages are drinks that are rich in carbon dioxide and have a distinctive, pleasant taste, refreshing properties and a bubbly quality.

Our bodies are made up of 60 % water. We drink every day to maintain our water balance. Some prefer coffee, some tea, juices and some carbonated drinks.

The fizzy, cheerful bubbles filling a glass of colourful drinks beckon us to taste them on a hot day. And advertising strongly invites us to "dip into the life-giving moisture" of refreshments. Very often from parents we hear the words: "Soda is bad, you can not drink it. Why is carbonated water sold in shops? Do all people think like our parents? Or maybe they just do not want to buy it? These questions have probably been asked more than once by different children. So we decided to find out if this is really the case and chose the topic of our study.

Modern mass culture and globalisation are unthinkable without soft drinks such as lemonade, Coke or Pepsi. In the US, the term softdrink is used to describe these types of drinks. Historian JudithJanko-Cogen, author of A History of Food. Major Inventions" notes that the soft drink industry emerged in the late 18th century, when carbon dioxide carbonated waters became available (in France and England). At the time it was considered an inexpensive imitation of medicinal mineral waters, with carbonated waters being sold in pharmacies rather than conventional shops. Further expansion was provided by chemists: in 1784 citric acid (from lemon juice) was isolated for the first time. In 1833, the first carbonated lemonades were sold in England[1].

Lemonade is of noble French origin (from limonade, which means "soft drink") and owes its origin to the mistake of King Louis I's court cupbearer, who, presenting the monarch with a wine glass, mixed up the wine and juice casks.

On the way to the royal table, having discovered his mistake, the cupbearer added mineral water to the juice and, bidding farewell to life, served the new drink to the king. The drink was to his majesty's liking and since then it has been known as "the king's lemonade" [14].

In 1850, Americans drank about 0.3 litres of carbonated drinks a year. Today, according to the National Soft Drinks Association, Americans consume more different drinks than water. In America, for every 0.4 litre of water consumed, 1.8 litres of carbonated drinks are consumed. The average male consumer between the ages of 12 and 19 drinks over two cans of carbonated beverages per day, or 868 cans per year. That is a lot. Let's look at the approximate composition of carbonated drinks. A 600-milliliter can of carbonated drink contains: carbonated water, natural or artificial flavorings, caffeine and 17 teaspoons of sugar. A 300-milliliter can contains 250 calories of caffeine, which affects the nervous system. According to a study published in November 2002 by the Journal of the American Medical Association, 24% of teenagers drink at least 0.7 litre of carbonated drinks a day. According to the Soft Drink Marketing Corporation, more than 2.5 billion litres of their products are consumed on average each year [17].

CHAPTER 1. CARBONATED DRINKS

1.1History of soda pop

We began our research by looking at the history of carbonated drinks.

Natural gassed water has been known since ancient times and has been used for medicinal purposes.

But it wasn't until the 17th century that someone enterprising came up with the idea of bottling water and selling it. This was also the time when the first sweet drinks appeared, but not yet carbonated.

Джозеф Пристли

In the 18th century, scientists realised what causes bubbles. And in 1767, English chemist Joseph Priestley figured out how to make ordinary water into carbonated water. At a meeting of physicists in London, he presented the world's first carbonated water machine. In Russia, the production of carbonated water began in the early 19th century in the suburbs of St. Petersburg. Initially it was soda water, which had a brackish taste and no therapeutic properties. Since then, carbonated water has not changed much and there is now a great variety of this water [15].

1.2 Chemical composition of carbonated drinks

We studied the labels on various carbonated water bottles and found that they contain carbon dioxide, sugar, colouring and flavouring agents, caffeine and preservatives [5, 9].

Carbon dioxide. Well soluble in water. It is used as a preservative. It is labelled E 290 on the product packaging. It is harmless on its own. But its presence in water excites gastric secretion, increases the acidity of gastric juice and provokes flatulence.

Sugar. Contained in almost all carbonated waters, in very large quantities. 3.5 to 6 sugars per glass. By quenching thirst for a few minutes, this very sweet water makes one drink much more than necessary. It is therefore impossible to get drunk with such water.

Aspartame. The sweetener E-951 aspartame is genetically a modified neurotoxin, used as an artificial sugar substitute. Aspartame is about 200 times sweeter than sugar, but in comparison it contains no carbohydrates or calories. Some researchers point out the chemical instability of aspartame. They say that after several weeks in hot climates or when heated to 300C, the bulk of aspartame in carbonated water breaks down into formaldehyde, methanol, phenylalanine and other substances. Scientists have stated that aspartame can cause kidney and peripheral nerve cancer. An unmistakable sign of aspartame is the warning: "Contains phenylalanine" or if the packaging mentions phenylketonuria, a congenital disorder of phenylalanine metabolism in the body leading to mental retardation.

Sodium benzoate. Preservative E-211 sodium benzoate, benzoic acid E- 210 and potassium benzoate E-212 are introduced into drinks as bactericidal and antifungal agents, increasing the shelf life of food several times over. Products containing sodium and calcium benzoates are not recommended for people with asthma or who are sensitive to aspirin. In combination with vitamin C, it releases benzene, which is a carcinogen.

Citric acid E-330 - added most often to carbonated drinks, it irritates the mucous membrane of the stomach and can lead to gastritis.

Orthophosphoric acid E-338 promotes calcium leaching from bones, calcium deficiency can cause osteoporosis. If the beverage has passed all levels of certification, it is likely that the level of acid is within tolerance and is not hazardous.

Caffeine. It is a mild nervous system stimulant. Children who drink a lot of caffeine are more restless, have trouble falling asleep and often suffer from headaches. Their ability to concentrate may be impaired. Caffeine is addictive.

Dyes are used to make the beverage look more beautiful and to make people want to buy and drink it. Dyes used in beverages can be natural or artificial. The most common natural colouring agent is sugar colouring E-150, i.e. burnt sugar. Artificial colouring agents are chemicals with specific properties that are far from useful. You should be especially careful with dyes that contain nitrogen (E-102, E-110, E-123, E-124, E-133, E-151).

Flavourings. These are the things that make us believe we are drinking something orange, apple, cherry or pear. Most flavourings are man-made chemicals, although plant-based drinks are also available.

So the whole value of a carbonated drink, which comes under dozens of brands, is in the water and carbon dioxide, and all the appeal is in the flavouring and the colouring.

CHAPTER 2. RESEARCH INTO THE KNOWLEDGE OF SCHOOLCHILDREN IN GRADES 6-11 OF CARBONATED BEVERAGES

2.1 A sociological survey among students

In order to achieve our goal, we decided to compile a questionnaire. Pupils in grades 6-11 (200 people) took part in the survey. The questionnaire was used to determine the popularity of carbonated water. The questionnaire was to find out the awareness of carbonated beverages. The following questions and answer options were offered:

1. Do you consume sugary carbonated drinks?
   a) yes b) no c) sometimes
2. If so, how often?
   a) every day b) once a week c) once a month d) not using
3. What carbonated drinks do you drink most often?
4. You consume carbonated drinks because
   a) tasty b) thirsty c) commercialsg) other
5. Did you know that carbonated drinks can harm your health?
   a) yes b) no c) difficult to answer
6. Does the colour of the carbonated drink make you uncomfortable?
   a) yes b) no c) difficult to answer

Analyzing the data from the sociological survey, we can say that pupils know that carbonated water is harmful, but still most of the children drink it. The students appreciate Lemonade, Coca-Cola, Sprite, Fanta, Pepsi, and Vita kvass.

The results of the survey are presented in diagrams 1 to 6

Diagram No. 1

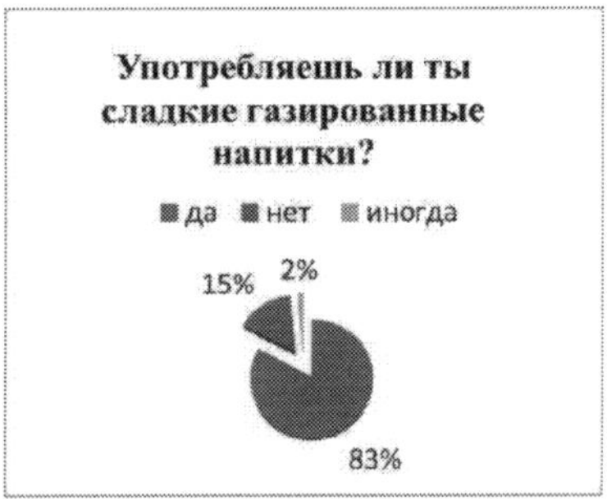

Diagram No. 2

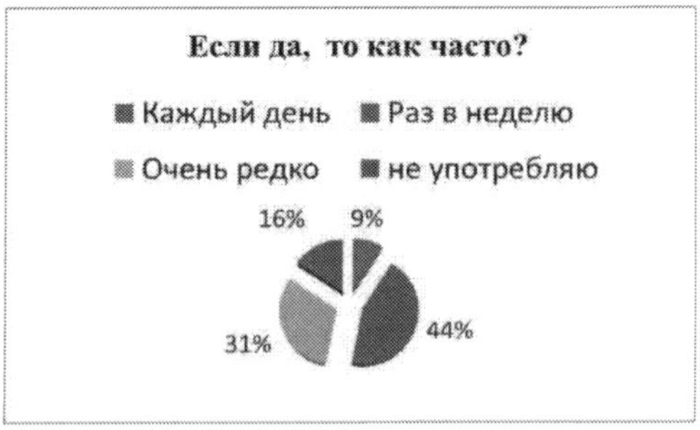

Diagram No. 3

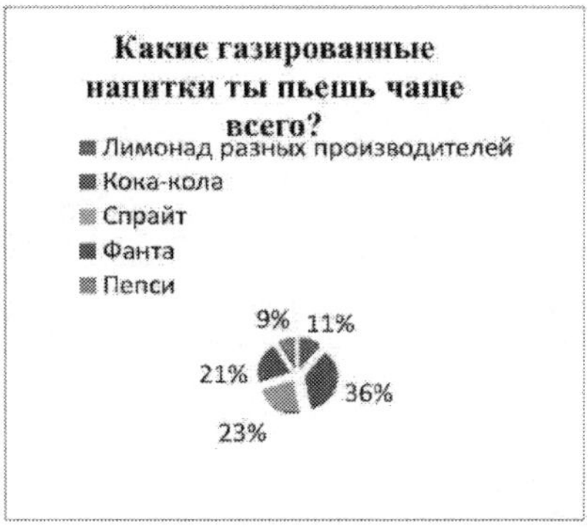

Diagram No. 4

Diagram No. 5

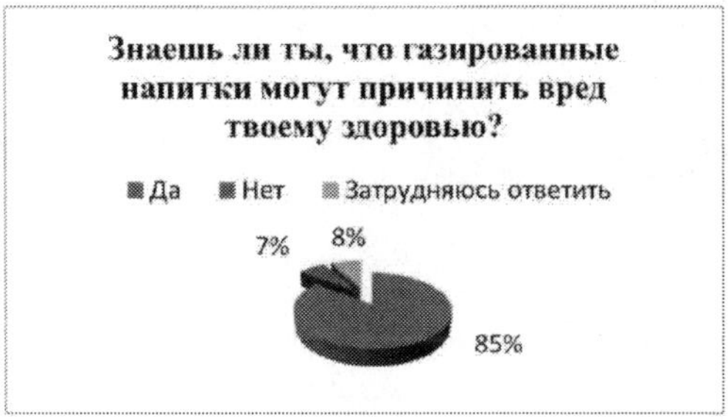

Diagram No. 6

Survey results

The majority of students (83%) in the survey like carbonated drinks, with 44% drinking it once a week.

85% of the students surveyed are aware of the dangers of carbonated drinks from parents, teachers and the media, but do not attach much importance to this information and therefore consume carbonated drinks.

The highest preference is for Coca-Cola (36%), Sprite (23%), Fanta (21%), Pepsi (11%) and lemonade from various manufacturers (20%). The choice of beverage is influenced by taste (54%) and thirst (27%). Many (54%) are not embarrassed by the bright colour of the drink, but are attracted to it.

It is not in vain that they say: "From the mouths of babes speaks the truth". It is necessary to listen to the younger generation, to their opinions and views on the issue raised in the research paper. After all, they are the future of the country and its potential. I would like to note that the answer option "find a decent alternative" reflects real steps to solve the urgent problem, such as: playing sports, organizing one's free time, controlling pricing policy, banning and restricting the production and export of carbonated beverages.

CHAPTER 3. RESEARCH ON THE CHEMICAL ANALYSIS OF CARBONATED DRINKS

3.1 Analysis of carbonated drinks by label

Before we understand whether carbonated drinks are harmful, let's find out what substances they contain. We analysed the labels of carbonated drinks and obtained the following data (Appendix 1).

The drinks were found to contain: carbon dioxide, citric and orthophosphoric acids, artificial flavours, flavourings, dyes, which can cause serious illness.

Photo No. 1 Samples of carbonated drinks to be analysed

Samples of carbonated drinks analysed: Mojito-flavoured Schweppes, Vita Bread Spike drink, SEVEN-UP Lemon, Lime and Bubbles, Fanta Orange, Pepsi, Sprite,Coca-Cola, Vita Duchesse drink, Pridvinje and Plum drink, Burn (energy drink).

3.2 Chemical analysis of carbonated drinks

3.2.1 Determination of carbon dioxide in samples using an air balloon

Study materials: carbonated drinks, a balloon.

How to do it: Place a balloon on the newly opened bottles.

Result: You saw that the balloons inflated instantly (Annex 2). *Conclusion:* carbonated drinks contain carbon dioxide.

3.2.2 Determination of carbon dioxide in carbonated drinks with lime water

Study materials: carbonated drinks, lime water.

How to proceed: Using a measuring cylinder, 10 ml each of the test beverage was poured into test tubes, sealed with a stopper with a gas escape tube and mounted on a rack. Lime water $Ca(OH)_2$ was poured into another test tube and the

end of the evacuation tube and gently heated it for 1 minute.
Observed the changes (Appendix 3).

Result: The lime water became cloudy in each of the proposed samples.

Table No. 1 Determination of carbon dioxide in carbonated drinks

Name of the drink	Clouding with t	Clouding without t
"Schweppes with Mojito Flavour	+	
Vita Bread Spike drink		+
"SEVEN-UP lemon, lime and bubbles"	+	
Fanta Orange	+	
Pepsi		+
Sprite		+
Coca-Cola		+
VitaDuchesse drink		+
Pridwine and plum drink	+ (2 min)	
Burn (energy drink)	+ (2 min)	

Conclusion: so there is carbonic acid in every beverage tested, which decomposes to release CO2, the presence of which has been proven by the turbidity of $Ca(OH)_2$. The presence of large amounts of carbon dioxide can cause flatulence and intestinal distress in the body.

3.2.3 Determination of the acidity of carbonated drinks (pH of the solution)

Examination materials: carbonated drinks, universal indicator paper.

Workflow: Beverage bottles were opened just before the experiment, poured into 10ml beakers, then indicator paper was added to all samples and their colouring was observed (Appendix 4).

Result: the universal indicator turned pink in all samples tested, and an increased acidity was noted (Table 2).

Table No. 2 Determining the acidity of carbonated drinks

Name of the drink	pH	Solution medium
"Schweppes with Mojito Flavour	2	sour
Vita Bread Spike drink	2	sour
"SEVEN-UP lemon, lime and bubbles"	2	sour
Fanta Orange	2	sour
Pepsi	2	sour
Sprite	2	sour
Coca-Cola	2	sour
Vita Duchesse drink	2	sour
Pridwine and plum drink	2	sour
Burn (energy drink)	1	sour

Conclusion: the change in indicator colouration confirms that acids are present as additives in all samples. This suggests that these drinks, being highly acidic in their solutions, may have a detrimental effect on the human gastrointestinal tract.

3.2.4 Effect of acidic carbonated beverage solutions on limestone

Materials for the study: carbonated drinks, limestone.

Procedure: Put the CaCO3 slices in the test tubes and add the beverage samples to be tested.

Result: Gas release and dissolution of calcium carbonate is observed (Appendix 5, Table No. 3).

Table No. 3 Effect of acidic carbonated drink solutions on limestone

Name of the drink	Carbon dioxide emission	Changing the colour of a carbonated drink
"Schweppes with Mojito Flavour	stormy	unchanged
Vita Bread Spike drink	very stormy	lightened
"SEVEN-UP lemon, lime and bubbles"	very stormy	unchanged
Fanta Orange	very stormy	pale
Pepsi	very stormy	lightened
Sprite	very stormy	unchanged
Coca-Cola	very stormy	lightened
Vita Duchesse drink	stormy	unchanged
Pridwine and plum drink	stormy	unchanged
Burn (energy drink)	very stormy	Lilac

Conclusion: The results confirm the presence of acids in the beverages tested, which can have a damaging effect on tooth enamel and the body's bone system.

3.2.5 The effect of carbonated drinks on a rusty nail

Study material: carbonated drinks, rusty nails.

Procedure: immerse a rusty nail in the beverage sample tubes and leave for 7 days (Annex 6, Table No. 4).

Result: We note that rust marks are less or no longer visible.

Table No. 4Effects of carbonated drinks on rusty nail

Name of the drink	Rust
"Schweppes with Mojito Flavour	a rusty nail shines
Vita Bread Spike drink	a rusty nail shines
"SEVEN-UP lemon, lime and bubbles"	a rusty nail shines
Fanta Orange	a rusty nail shines
Pepsi	the rusty nail is shiny, the sludge has fallen
Sprite	a rusty nail shines
Coca-Cola	the rusty nail is shiny, the sludge has fallen
Vita Duchesse drink	a rusty nail shines
Pridwine and plum drink	a rusty nail shines
Burn (energy drink)	a rusty nail shines

*Conclusion:*Carbonated water has phosphoric acid, which reacts and removes rust and household pollutants.

3.2.6 Determining the presence of colouring agents in carbonated drinks

Examination materials: carbonated drinks (50 ml each), activated charcoal (0.5 g each)

Study time: 30 minutes.

Workflow: 50 ml of the test carbonated drink was poured into chemical beakers and 0.5 g of activated carbon was added to each beaker, stirred thoroughly, allowed to stand for 30 minutes and the contents of the beaker was shaken every 5 minutes. Afterwards the charcoal was filtered off. The degree of adsorption was determined visually from the colour intensity (Appendix 7).

Result: During the experiment, we obtained the following data in Table 5.

Table No. 5Determination of colouring agents in carbonated drinks

Name of the drink	Time	Result
"Schweppes with Mojito Flavour	30 minutes	complete adsorption
Vita Bread Spike drink	30 minutes	complete adsorption
"SEVEN-UP lemon, lime and bubbles"	30 minutes	complete adsorption
Fanta Orange	30 minutes	complete adsorption
Pepsi	30 minutes	complete adsorption
Sprite	30 minutes	complete adsorption
Coca-Cola	30 minutes	complete adsorption
Vita Duchesse drink	30 minutes	complete adsorption
Pridwine and plum drink	30 minutes	complete adsorption
Burn (energy drink)	30 minutes	complete adsorption

Conclusion: It can thus be proved that the drinks in question contain dyes. The dyes in carbonated drinks are artificial because they are well adsorbed, unlike natural ingredients. These colours can alter the colour of teeth.

3.2.7 Effect of carbonated drink dyes on eggshells

Materials for the study: carbonated drinks, eggshells.

Study time: 30 minutes.

Procedure: Egg shells were placed in beakers with carbonated beverage samples and left for 30 minutes. The egg shells were observed to change in colour and break down (Appendix 8).

Result: The eggshells stain in the solutions after 30 minutes.

Table No. 6The influence of colourants in carbonated drinks on eggshells

Name of the drink	Shell colouring
"Schweppes with Mojito Flavour	the shell is not stained
Vita Bread Spike drink	the shell is more intensely coloured
"SEVEN-UP lemon, lime and bubbles"	the shell is not stained
Fanta Orange	the shell is lightly stained
Pepsi	the shell is more intensely coloured
Sprite	the shell is not stained
Coca-Cola	the shell is more intensely coloured
Vita Duchesse drink	the shell is not stained
Pridwine and plum drink	the shell is not stained
Burn (energy drink)	the shell is more intensely coloured

Conclusion: The change in egg shell colouration confirms the presence of dyes in the beverages tested. The staining of the eggshells shows that the teeth can also become stained when drinking these drinks.Consumption of carbonated drinks in large quantities can lead to calcium dissolving (teeth, nails) and tooth enamel destruction.

3.2.8 Effects of dyes in carbonated drinks on capron fabric

Study material: carbonated drinks, a piece of capron cloth.

Procedure: put a small piece of capron cloth in each beverage sample test tube and leave it for 1 day (Annex 9, Table 7).

Table No. 7The effect of carbonated drink colourants on napron tissue

Name of the drink	Dyeing the capron fabric
"Schweppes with Mojito Flavour	the kapron fabric is not stained
Vita Bread Spike drink	the kapron fabric is dyed more intensively
"SEVEN-UP lemon, lime and bubbles"	the kapron fabric is not dyed
Fanta Orange	the kapron fabric is dyed more intensively
Pepsi	the kapron fabric is dyed more intensively
Sprite	the kapron fabric is not dyed
Coca-Cola	the kapron fabric is dyed more intensively
Vita Duchesse drink	the kapron fabric is not stained
Pridwine and plum beverage	the kapron fabric is not dyed
Burn (energy drink)	the kapron fabric is dyed more intensively

Conclusion: The change in the colouration of the capron tissue confirms the presence of dyes in the beverages tested. The staining of the capron tissue shows that the teeth can also be stained when drinking these drinks.

3.2.9 Effects of the acidic environment of carbonated drinks on fats

Study material: carbonated drinks, animal fat.

Procedure: place a small piece of lard each in beverage cups and leave at room temperature for 1 day (Appendix 10, Table 8).

Table No. 8The influence of the acidic environment of carbonated drinks on fats

Name of the drink	Result
"Schweppes with Mojito Flavour	staining has not occurred
Vita Bread Spike drink	staining is strong
"SEVEN-UP lemon, lime and bubbles"	staining has not occurred
Fanta Orange	staining has not occurred
Pepsi	staining is strong
Sprite	staining has not occurred
Coca-Cola	staining is strong
Vita Duchesse drink	staining has not occurred
Pridwine and plum drink	staining has not occurred
Burn (energy drink)	staining is strong

Conclusion: the substances in the drink have a destructive effect on organic substances, particularly fats, and therefore can also have a harmful effect on the human body if consumed.

3.2.10 Effects of acidic carbonated beverages on soft tissue

Study material: carbonated drinks, pieces of meat (beef).

How to proceed: put a small piece of meat in each beverage sample test tube and leave it at room temperature for 1 day (Appendix 11).

Result: A disgusting transformation of a piece of meat (table 9).

Conclusion: substances in carbonated water can corrode soft tissue.

Table No. 9 Effect of acidic carbonated drinks on soft tissue

Name of the drink	Result
"Schweppes with Mojito Flavour	decomposition
Vita Bread Spike drink	decomposition
"SEVEN-UP lemon, lime and bubbles"	decomposition
Fanta Orange	decomposition, staining
Pepsi	decomposition
Sprite	decomposition
Coca-Cola	Decomposition, precipitation
Vita Duchesse drink	decomposition
Pridwine and plum drink	decomposition
Burn (energy drink)	decomposition

3.2.11 Determination of the naturalness of the drinks to be analysed

The naturalness of the beverages examined was determined by the colour change of the soda after boiling it with baking soda for 10 minutes: if the coloured beverage did not change its original colour, then the beverage is completely chemical. The colour change of the soda can be considered an indication of the naturalness of the drink (Appendix 12, Table 10).

Table No. 10 Results of naturalness of the sodas analysed
("-"-no visible change; "+"-significant change in colour;
"++"-significant change in colour)

Name of the drink	Result
"Schweppes with Mojito Flavour	+
Vita Bread Spike drink	- —
"SEVEN-UP lemon, lime and bubbles"	- —
Fanta Orange	+
Pepsi	- —
Sprite	- —
Coca-Cola	- —
Vita Duchesse drink	- —
Pridwine and plum drink	- —
Burn (energy drink)	++ (turned blue)

Conclusion: the most 'natural' of the drinks analysed are Schweppes Mojito Flavour, Fanta (which contains 3% orange juice), Vigp (an energy drink).

3.2.12 Detection of phosphoric acid in carbonated drinks

Test tubes were filled with 10 ml each of the carbonated beverages tested. Each test tube was heated to a boil to remove the dissolved carbon dioxide in the solution. Then a few drops of silver nitrate solution were added to each test tube and if a precipitate of silver orthophosphate appeared, it could be concluded that the drink contained orthophosphoric acid (Appendix 13, Table 11):

$$H3PO4 + 3AgNO3 = Ag3PO4 + 3HNO3$$

Table No. 11Results for orthophosphoric acid in carbonated drinks

Name of the drink	Result
"Schweppes with Mojito Flavour	+
Vita Bread Spike drink	- —
"SEVEN-UP lemon, lime and bubbles"	- —
Fanta Orange	- (turned black)
Pepsi	- —
Sprite	+
Coca-Cola	- —
Vita Duchesse drink	- —
Pridwine and plum drink	- —
Burn (energy drink)	+ (turned brown, lost transparency)

Conclusion: In a chemical experiment, we verified that the Schweppes Mojito, Sprite, Burn (an energy drink) contains orthophosphoric acid, as a white precipitate of silver phosphate precipitated in the test tubes.

3.2.13Compatibility study for carbonated beverages and mints

This part of the work was prompted by media reports that cases of teenagers drinking carbonated drinks and mints together had emerged. The media reported that not only the various chemical additives, but also the carbon dioxide that is abundantly released when these substances interact (up to and including death), were damaging to health.

For this part of the work, 1 piece of Na1I candy was added to ten samples of carbonated water (Annex 14, Table 12). (Appendix 14, Table 12).

Table No. 12 Results of interaction between drinks and lollipops ("-"-no visible change; "+"-slight gas emission;
"+++"- abundant gas emission)

Name of the drink	Result
"Schweppes with Mojito Flavour	+
Vita Bread Spike drink	+
"SEVEN-UP lemon, lime and bubbles"	+
Fanta Orange	+
Pepsi	+
Sprite	+
Coca-Cola	+
Vita Duchesse drink	+
Pridwine and plum drink	-—
Burn (energy drink)	-—

Conclusion: carbonated drinks, with the exception of Pridvinieris Plum and Burn (an energy drink), are more likely than other sodas to interact with lollipops, which can be detrimental to the health of adolescents.

Conclusions: The results of the study lead us to the conclusion that solutions of acids, such as orthophosphoric acid, are added to carbonated beverages. In addition to the main ingredients, many beverages have food additives that help preserve the product (preservatives), flavour it (flavourings), colour it (colourings) and sweeten it. Many of them are the work of chemists and are derived from synthetic substances.

So, having studied the composition and some of the properties of carbonated drinks, and analysing the results of a sociological survey, the following conclusions can be drawn:

- When choosing carbonated drinks, pupils are guided by organoleptic properties (taste, aroma, colour), cost and least of all by the contents of the label.
- all of the drinks tested contain large amounts of carbon dioxide;
- all of the beverages under study have a higher acidity of solutions;
- soda water has phosphoric acid, which reacts and removes rust and household contaminants.
- all the drinks tested contain artificial colours and flavourings

The drinks offered by manufacturers, due to the harmful additives they contain, can cause serious health problems, so you should pay attention to their composition before drinking them.

Thus, after conducting experiments and studying the components of carbonated water, we are convinced that its excessive consumption leads to a variety of diseases, such as: gastritis; stomach ulcers; allergies; tooth decay; kidney stones and others.

So, the main enemies from a carbonated bottle for our bodies are:

- sugar, which can be as much as 5 spoonfuls per glass;
- carbohydrates and carbon dioxide;
- colourings and flavourings that put a strain on the liver;
- caffeine - which excites the nervous system;
- preservatives - irritating to the gastric mucosa.

CHAPTER 4 CONCLUSION

After analyzing experiments and studies and studying the literature, we were convinced that carbonated drinks contain a chemical reaction that worsens our health. Once in our body these drinks change their composition, they contain many dyes, they leave plaque on our teeth and tongue, which leads to tooth decay, and they also contain a lot of sugar, which is also harmful to our body. We found out that:

- sugary carbonated drinks do not quench our thirst, although that is what we buy them for.
- The chemical composition of the drinks has a devastating effect on health: teeth are destroyed, bones become brittle, obesity, allergies and stomach problems can occur.
- It is best to use morsels, mineral water, purified drinking water and juices to quench your thirst.
- As a result of our work, we have concluded that carbonated drinks have a negative effect on the human body, so our hypothesis is fully confirmed.

It's safe to say about carbonated drinks: they are damaging to the body. So anyone who is serious about their health and weight should say NO to carbonated drinks and drink lots of water. A lot of carbonated drinks means a lot of calories. So it's no surprise that carbonated drinks are the fifth biggest source of calories for adults.

Health experts cite carbonated drinks among the factors responsible for reducing the nutrients in our diets. Firstly, sugary teas and 'sports drinks' replace the nutrients found in milk and juice. Secondly, although these drinks are high in calories, they do nothing to reduce appetite, so we end up with a double dose of calories each day, and this contributes to the obesity epidemic [7, 8].

Also, excessive consumption of sugar-rich soft drinks has a negative impact on the mental state of adolescents [13].

Researchers have found that young people who drink soda more often than others are more prone to hyperactivity and are also more likely to be stressed, while young people who do not drink soda are more mentally resilient than those who drink it regularly [6].

Having carried out this research work and studied the chemical composition of carbonated drinks and their effects on the human body, the following conclusions can be drawn:

- sugary carbonated drinks do more harm than good;
- They lead to gastrointestinal diseases, kidney disease and allergies;

- increase the likelihood of obesity and diabetes mellitus;
- lead to addiction and, if used for a long time, can cause cancer.

Forward work plan

We plan to share the conclusions of the research work with the students at the school. We think that in the future they will be more careful about what they consume as drinks. We believe that our work will be of interest not only to the students, but also to their parents, because a careful attitude towards one's health should be developed from an early age. Then taking care of one's health will become a natural form of behaviour in the future. Otherwise we will all continue to consume not what the body needs, but what the most successful advertisers offer us.

Work on the research on sodas can continue: making fruit essences and carbonated drinks independently; determining the content of colourings, heavy metals in sodas, etc.

Buyer tips

After studying this material, we became convinced that carbonated water is harmful. We then decided to compile tips for customers:

1. Drink soda only on special occasions, not every day.
2. Don't keep carbonated drinks at home.
3. Think of a soda as a treat you can have on some kind of holiday.
4. Yellow and orange coloured drinks are particularly harmful. If you do decide to buy water, choose colourless water without any colourants.
5. If you drink soda, it is better to let the gases out.
6. If you want to save your teeth, drink through a straw.
7. Before buying, do not be lazy - study the label. Give preference to drinks made on a natural basis.
8. Soda does not quench thirst. The more you drink it, the more thirsty you get.

Advice on choosing safe drinks:

1. You should read the label carefully.
2. It's better to choose beverages with low-bright natural colours - there's a better chance of using natural dye.
3. Sugar-containing drinks are clearly preferable to sweetener-based drinks. Sweeteners are especially not recommended in pregnancy, high blood pressure and phenylketonuria.
4. Drinks containing sweeteners should not be kept out of the fridge, let alone heated.
5. Under no circumstances should you consume drinks with an expiry date.

List of references

1. Boryaev, V.E. Functional foodstuffs: Textbook /.
B. E. Boryaev. - Belgorod: Cooperative Education, 2005. - 130 c.
2. The impact of carbonated drinks on adolescents [Electronic resource] / SlideServe. - Access mode: https://www.slideserve.com/lindley/2985575. - Access

date: 27.12.2017.

3. The whole truth about carbonated drinks [Electronic resource] / MIRSOVETOV. - Access mode: http://mirsovetov.ru/a/medicine/nutrition/soda-water.html. - Access date: 26.12.2017.

4. Genetically modified sweetener [Electronic resource] / Nutrasweet/Aspartame. - Access mode: http://www.seu.ru/cci/campaign/gen/gmp.htm. - Access date: 28.12.2017.

5. Igosheva, E.V. How to recognize the composition of energy drinks / E.V. Igosheva, N.N. Trapeznikova - Journal of Chemistry at School. - № 8. - 2011. - C. 50-52.

6. Izhogina, E.Y. Energetics: all pros and cons / E.Y. Izhogina // Classroom teacher's companion. - 2009. - № 5. - C. 64-67

7. Internet magazine "Diagnosis", section "Medical articles", gastroenterologist I.V. Senchenko, "Carbonated drinks: harm and benefit", 2009.

8. Health" online magazine, "Healthy Lifestyle" section, article "Rational therapeutic diet", 2009.

9. Online magazine "School of Life", article by O. Antonov "What carbonated drinks contain", 2006.

10. Luc, E. Preservatives in food industry: Textbook for universities / E. Luc, M. Jaeger. - Ed. 3 revised and extended. - St. Petersburg: GIORD, 2004. - 256 c.

11. Pozdnyakovsky, V.N. Expertise of drinks: Textbook / V.N. Pozdnyakova. - Novosibirsk: Novosibirsk University,1999. - 305c.

12. Poznyakovsky, V.M. Expertise of drinks / V.M. Poznyakovsky, V.A. Pomozova et al. - Novosibirsk: Sib. univ. izd vo, 2002. - 384 c.

13. Popova, M. Energy drinks: energy comes out sideways / M. Popova // IA Interfax-West. - 2008. - C. 22-27.

14. Rodina, T.G. Tasting Analysis of Products: Textbook / T.G. Rodina, G.A. Vukes. - Moscow: Kolos, 2004. - 192 c.

15. Rudolf, V.V. Production of soft drinks and bottling of mineral water / V.V. Rudolf. Rudolf, V.E. Balashov. - Moscow: Agropromizdat, 1988. - 287 c.

16. Article "Public Awareness of Food Additives" / Biologiya Gazeta. - № 44, 2002.

17. Functional Foods: Textbook / Edited by Prof. V.I. Teplova. Belgorod: Cooperative Education, 2005. - 100 c.

18. Schuman, G. Soft drinks: raw materials, technologies, standards / G. Schuman. - SPb.: Profession, 2004. - 278 c.

19. Expertise of drinks: Practical work edited by V.M. Poznyakovsky. - Novosibirsk: Novosibirsk University Press,2002. - 334 c.

Annex 1

Analysis of carbonated drink labels

"SEVEN-UP lemon, lime and bubbles" 0.5l

Non-alcoholic carbonated beverage flavoured with Seven-Up

Ingredients: water, sugar, acidity regulator citric acid, natural flavouring, acidity regulators: E331 (i) and malic acid, preservative sodium benzoate, sweeteners sucralose and acesulfame potassium. Process auxiliary agent is used (contains water-holding agents: propylene glycol and glycerine, flavouring, acidity regulator citric acid).

Nutritional value of 100 ml, mean values: carbohydrates - 7.4 g, energy value - 29.6 kcal / 123.9kJ.

Manufactured using the technology of PepsiCo Inc. 7UP and the image of the 7UP logo are trademarks of Seven-Up International. Manufacturer: OJSC "Lidskoe Beer", Republic of Belarus, 231300, Grodno region, Lida, 32 Mickiewicza street.

EAS STB 539 Food Safety Management System FSSC 22000

Non-alcoholic carbonated drink "SWEPS WITH MOHITO Flavour" 0.5L

Ingredients: water, sugar, lime juice 3%, natural flavourings, acidity regulators (citric acid, sodium citrate), preservative potassium sorbate, stabilisers (gum arabic, glycerine and resin acid esters). Natural ingredients are allowed to precipitate.

Nutritional value 100 ml drink, 0 g protein, 0 g fat, 10.6 g carbohydrates, Total sugars - 10.6g, sodium < 16mg, energy value (calories) - 184 kJ / 44 Kcal.

Manufactured with the permission of Schweppes Holdings Limited by the unitary enterprise Coca-Cola Beverages Belarus.

Legal address: 147/2, Koliadichi village, Minsk district, Republic of Belarus, 223056. Registered address: 147/2, Koliadichi v., Koliadichi, Minsk district, Republic of Belarus, 223056. All rights reserved. ARTICLE 100373962/009-2014

Vita Bread Spike drink 0.5 l.

Non-alcoholic carbonated beverage with flavours, sweeteners "Vita. Duchesse" with preservative.

Ingredients: artesian water, complex food additive "Kvas": natural flavourings, stabilizers - gum arabic, dietary iodised salt; complex food additive: mix of sweeteners (aspartame, acesulfame potassium, sodium cyclamate, sodium saccharinade); acidity regulator - citric acid,

The preservative is sodium benzoate. The drink contains a source of phenylalanine.

Nutritional value: carbohydrates 0g/100cm3, energy value 1.0cal/100cm3 (4.18kJ/100cm3).

Manufacturer: JLLC "Vitebsk Soft Drinks Plant", 155 Leningradskaya street, Vitebsk, 210013, Republic of Belarus. Trade mark "Vita" under license of CJSC "Ricor" STB 539

Composition of Coca-Cola: water, sugar, caffeine, orthophosphoric acid, high fructose corn syrup, coca extract, cola nut extract, lemon extract, vanilla and glycerine.

Protein:0.00 g. Fats: 0.00 g. Carbohydrates: 10.60 g. Calorie content of 100 g food: 42.00 kcal

Composition of Fanta Orange: purified carbonated water, sugar, 3% orange juice, acidity regulator citric acid, antioxidant ascorbic acid, natural flavourings, stabilisers (glycerine and resin esters, guar gum), colourant beta-carotene.

Calories, kcal: 48
Protein, g: 0.0
Fats, g: 0.0
Carbohydrates, g: 11.7

Composition of Sprite: water, sugar, carbon dioxide, acidity regulators (citric acid, sodium citrate), natural flavourings, sweeteners (aspartame, acesulfame potassium), preservative (sodium benzonate). Protein: 0.10 g. Fats: 0.00g. Carbohydrates: 7,00 г.

Calorie content of 100 g food: 29.00 kcal

Composition of Pepsi: treated drinking water, sugar, carbon dioxide, natural colouring agent sugar tint, acidity regulator: orthophosphoric acid, caffeine, stabiliser gum arabic, natural flavouring.

Calorie content of 100 g of food: 38.

Protein, g: 0.0 Fats, g: 0.0 Carbohydrates, g: 8.7

Non-alcoholic strong carbonated energy drink - Burn

Ingredients: Water, sugar, acidity regulators (citric acid, sodium citrate), taurine, glucuronolactone, colourants(anthocyanins, sugar tint IV), preservatives (potassium sorbate, sodium benzoate), flavourings, caffeine, vitamin(PP(niacin), pantothenic acid, B6, B12), inositol, antioxidant ascorbic acid, guarana extract. Caffeine content max. 40mg/100ml.

Not recommended for use in children under 18 years of age, during pregnancy and lactation or in persons suffering from hyperexcitability, insomnia or arterial hypertension.

Nutritional value per 100ml: carbohydrates - 13.2g, total sugars - 13.2g, fat - 0g, vitamin PP (niacin) - 5.8mg, pantothenic acid - 1.1mg, vitamin B6 -0.6mg, vitamin B12-0 .28mg,
The energy value (calories) is 230 kJ (55 kcal).

Manufacturer: IP Coca-Cola Beverages Ukraine Limited, Ukraine, 07442 Kyiv region, Brovarsky district, V. Dymerka settlement, 51 km St.Peterburgskoe highway. Importer, authorized by the manufacturer in the Republic of Belarus: Unitary enterprise Coca-Cola Beverages Belarus. 223056, Republic of Belarus, Minsk region, v. Kolyadichi, 147/2. Tel: +375172100210

Pridvinje (butterscotch and plum)

Ingredients: drinking water, sugar, food additives: acidity regulator - citric acid, flavouring - sodium benzoate, acidity regulator - sodium citrate, lemon-lime flavouring, food additive: flavour and aroma enhancer E636. Energy value - 130 kJ (30 kcal)/100ml. (The composition is a sticker on top of the main composition. Shelf life 180 days. Store at temperatures between 0 and 22 degrees Celsius. "Vitebsk Distillery "Pridvinje" 210001 Vitebsk. Vitebsk, 45 Revolutsionnaya str.

BITA Duchesse

Ingredients: artesian water, Duchesse flavouring; complex food additive Chocolate Colour Solution (natural): sugar colouring agent (natural), preservative potassium sorbate; complex food additive: mix of sweeteners (sodium cyclamate, asapatame, sodium saccharinate, potassium acesulfame); acidity regulator - citric acid; preservative - sodium benzoate. Contains a source of phenylalanine.

Nutritional value: carbohydrates - 0g/100cm3, energy value - 0.7 kcal/100cm3 (2.93 kJ/100cm3). Store at an ambient temperature between 0 and 22 degrees Celsius. Shelf life - no more than 180 days. Non alcoholic carbonated beverage with aromas and sweeteners "Vrga. Duchesse" with preservative. Manufacturer: JLLC "Vitebsk Soft Drinks Plant" 210013, Republic of Belarus, Vitebsk, 155 Leningradskaya street, tel: (0212)620205. Trademark "Vgga" under license of CJSC "Rikor".

Annex 2

Determination of carbon dioxide in samples using a balloon

Annex 3

Determination of carbon dioxide in samples using lime water

"Schweppes Mojito-flavoured" Limestone Beverage Vita Bread Spike

"SEVEN-UP lemon, lime and bubbles"

Fanta Orange

Pepsi

Sprite

Coca-Cola

VitaDuchesse drink

Pridvinje and Pridvinje and Pridvinje plum drink

Burn (energy drink)

Annex 4

Determining the acidity of carbonated drinks

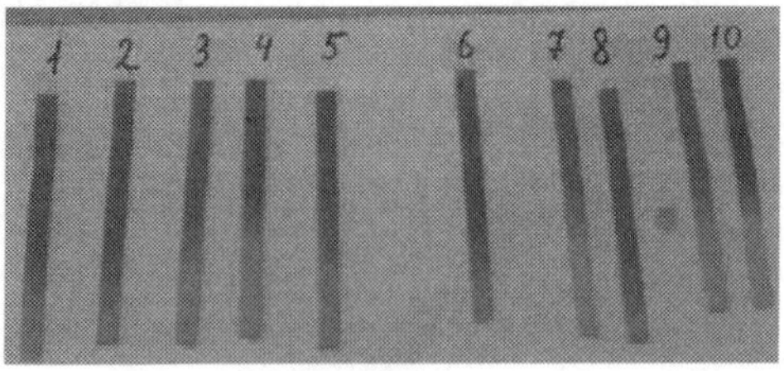

Annex 5

Effect of acidic carbonated beverage solutions on limestone

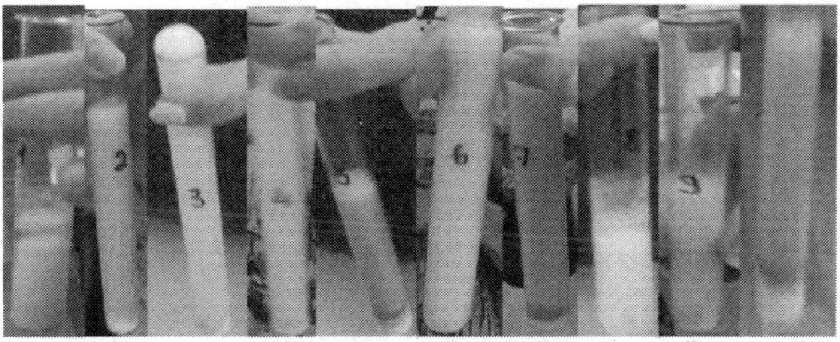

1 2 3 4 5 6 7 8 9 10

1. "Schweppes with Mojito Flavour
2. Vita Bread Spike drink
3. "SEVEN-UP lemon, lime and bubbles"
4. Fanta Orange
5. Pepsi
6. Sprite
7. Coca-Cola
8. Vita Duchesse drink
9. Pridvinje and Pridvinje and Pridvinje Plum" drink
10. Burn (energy drink)

Annex *6*
The effect of carbonated drinks on a rusty nail

Before the experiment

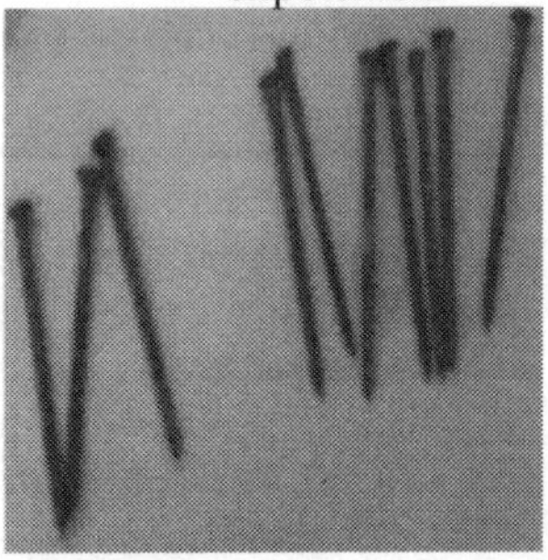

After the experiment

Annex 7

Determining the presence of colouring agents in carbonated drinks

Determination of dyes in samples

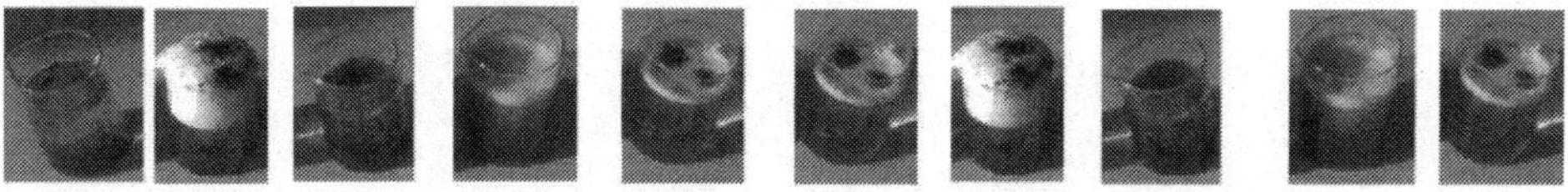

1 2 3 4 5 6 7 8 9 10

Result of adsorption

1. "Schweppes with Mojito Flavour
2. Vita Bread Spike drink
3. "SEVEN-UP lemon, lime and bubbles"
4. Fanta Orange
5. Pepsi
6. Sprite
7. Coca-Cola
8. Vita Duchesse drink
9. Pridvinje and Pridvinje and Pridvinje Plum" drink
10. Burn (energy drink)

Annex 8

Effect of dyes in carbonated drinks on eggshells

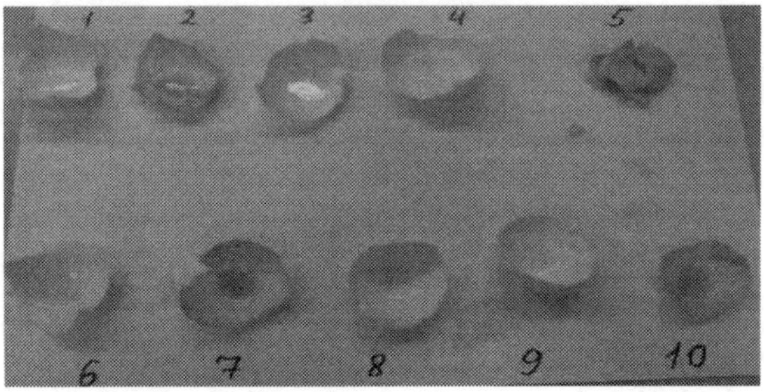

Annex 9

Influence of carbonated drink dyes on capron fabric

1. "Schweppes with Mojito Flavour
2. Vita Bread Spike drink
3. "SEVEN-UP lemon, lime and bubbles"
4. Fanta Orange
5. Pepsi
6. Sprite
7. Coca-Cola
8. Vita Duchesse drink
9. Pridvinje and Pridvinje and Pridvinje Plum" drink

Before the After the experiment

10. Burn (energy drink)

Annex 10

Effect of the acidic environment of carbonated drinks on fats

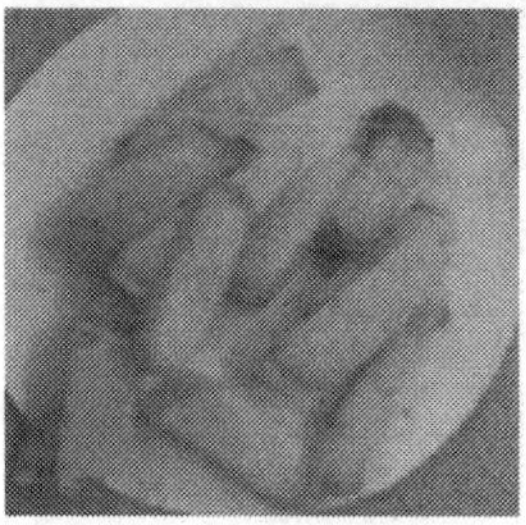

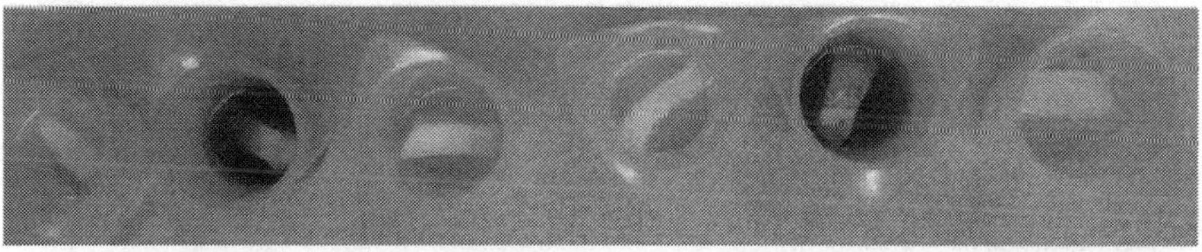

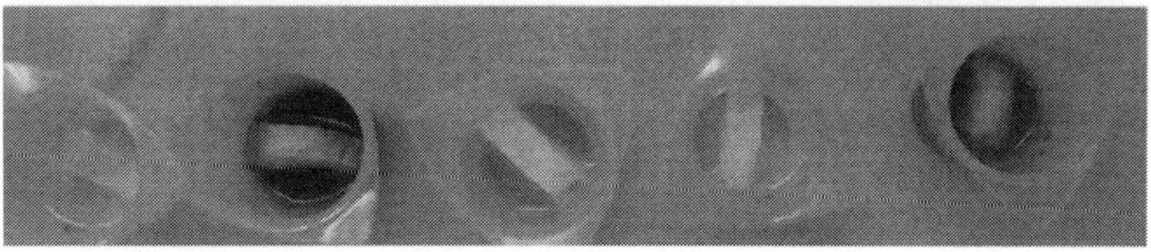

Annex 11

Effects of acidic carbonated drinks on soft tissue

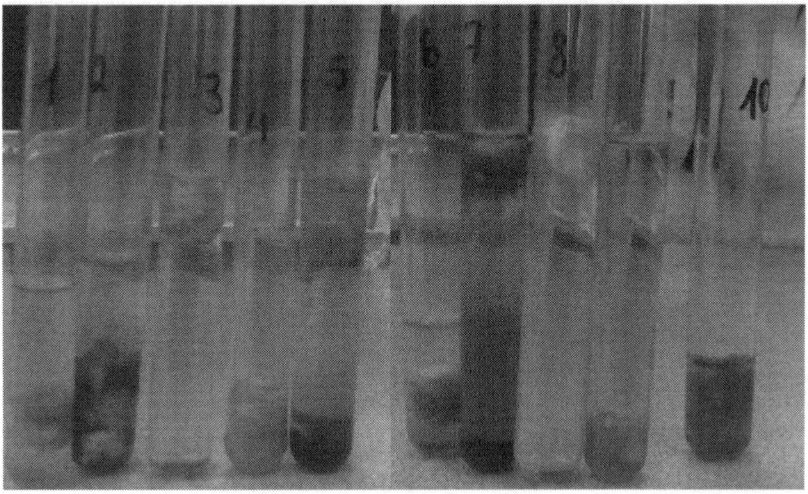

Annex 12 **Definition of naturalness beverages**

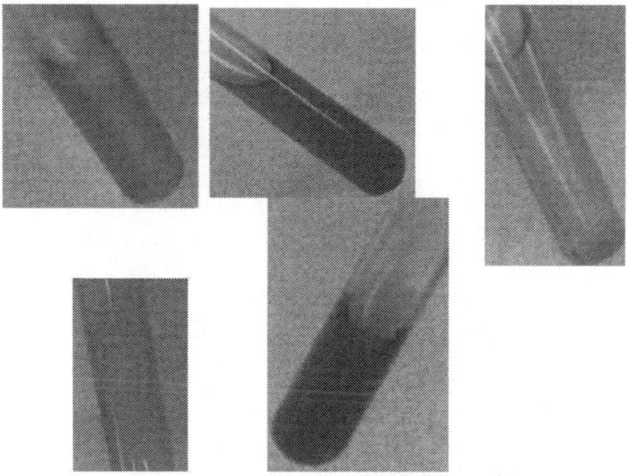

1 2 3 4 5

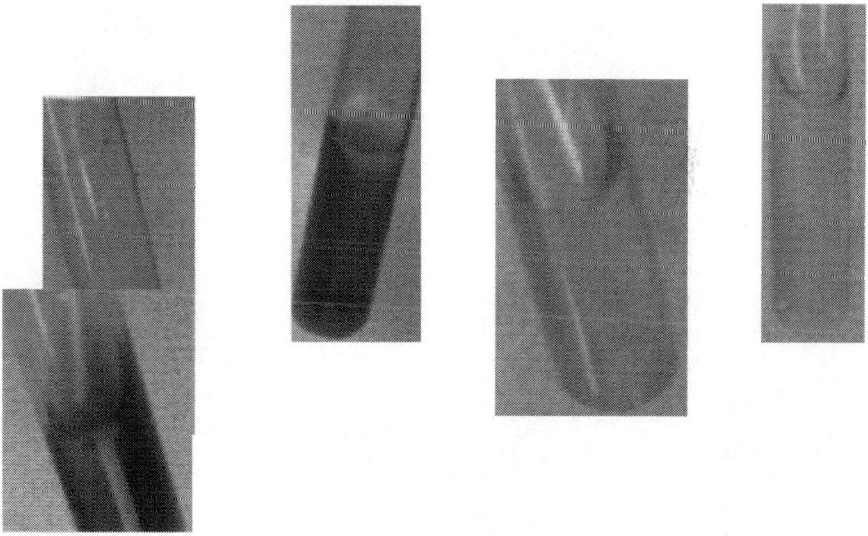

678 9 10

1. "Schweppes with Mojito Flavour

2. Vita Bread Spike drink
3. "SEVEN-UP lemon, lime and bubbles"
4. Fanta Orange
5. Pepsi
6. Sprite
7. Coca-Cola
8. Vita Duchesse drink
9. Pridvinje and Pridvinje and Pridvinje Plum" drink
10. Burn (energy drink)

Annex 13

Detection of phosphoric acid in carbonated drinks

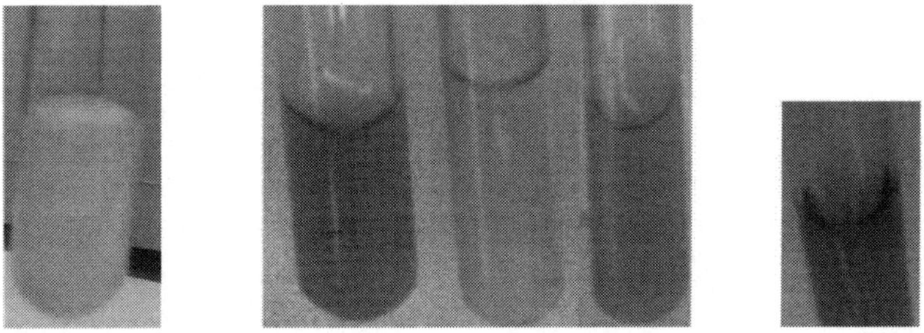

1 2 3 4 5

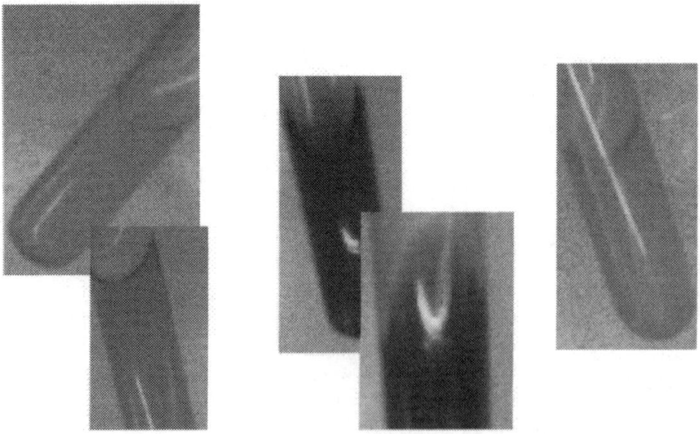

6 7 8 9 10

1. "Schweppes with Mojito Flavour
2. Vita Bread Spike drink
3. "SEVEN-UP lemon, lime and bubbles"
4. Fanta Orange
5. Pepsi
6. Sprite
7. Coca-Cola
8. VitaDuchesse drink
9. Drink "Pridvinjeiriso". plum "
10. Burn (energy drink)

Annex 14

A study of carbonated drinks and mints compatibility (candy)

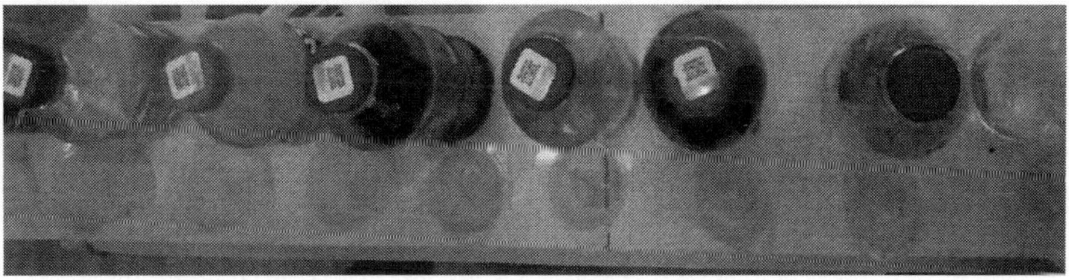

Annex 15

Effects of carbonated drink ingredients on human health

The most serious consequences of regular and frequent consumption of carbonated drinks are digestive diseases; obesity, diabetes and tooth decay; urolithiasis and urolithiasis; allergies. It is absolutely contraindicated for pre-school children and children suffering from any type of gastritis, gastroduodenitis, predisposition to diabetes mellitus or urolithiasis. It is strictly forbidden to drink fizzy drinks on an empty stomach. It is better to replace it with dairy products and natural juices.

Sugars and other chemicals in them 'trick' the brain into giving it pleasure devoid of benefits. Excess sugar burns up extra B vitamins and leads to obesity and diabetes. But that's not the main point, because sweet foods are plentiful. Sweet fizzy drinks contain citric, malic or orthophosphoric acid, which damages the mucous membrane of the gastrointestinal tract, and also gradually dissolves tooth enamel, washing out the calcium. The same process occurs in the bones. So drinking carbonated drinks on a regular basis over a long period of time may stimulate the development of osteoporosis. Most carbonated drinks, unfortunately, do not quench thirst, but rather excite it. This is because they all contain either very high levels of sugar (10 to 15 g per 100 ml), or sugar substitutes (aspartame, cyclamate, saccharine). Both sugar and food additives - sweeteners leave a sugary aftertaste, which has to be drunk again and again. If a child drinks a lot of soda, the pancreas is put under considerable strain, which can lead to a disease such as diabetes mellitus. In addition to sweet additives many fizzy drinks contain caffeine (approx. 10 mg per 100 ml) and quinine, citric acid (E 330) and orthophosphoric acid (E 338). The phosphorous salts in the soda form insoluble and completely indigestible compounds with the calcium, which are rapidly removed from the body. This has an adverse effect on the formation of the child's bone tissue. Calcium deficiency may also manifest itself as excessive excitability, insomnia, irritability, sore gums, slow growth. All carbonated drinks contain preservatives, sodium benzoate (E 211) or potassium sorbitol (E 202), as well as colourings and flavourings. All these substances, as well as the gases themselves, have an adverse effect on the mucous membrane of the entire digestive tract. Dyes, preservatives, flavourings and other additives contained in coloured carbonated soft drinks also have an adverse effect on the health of the child. In addition to allergic reactions, they can lead to so-called "hyperactivity and attention deficit syndrome". Children with this syndrome find it more difficult to learn. So it is clear that carbonated drinks, if consumed very frequently, can have a negative impact on health. So a little precaution does not hurt.

Some people prefer coffee, tea, juice and morsels, while others prefer carbonated drinks. The question of how harmful carbonated water is to human health, and especially to children, has been discussed in the world for a very long time. During that time, scientists have conducted a number of studies showing that today the number of young people suffering from osteoporosis, i.e. reduced bone density, has increased dramatically. The cause of this dangerous disease is a lack of calcium in the body, which people get from consuming milk, cheese and cottage cheese. Taking into account the peculiarities of today's youth, who prefer carbonated water to milk, it is clear that most of today's children lack calcium, which increases the natural process of bone destruction that begins in humans after the age of 22.

We drink sugary carbonated drinks without thinking about the damage they can do to our bodies. And the harm is considerable, as consumers' rights groups in many countries point out. The additional sugar intake from soft drinks causes at least 4 undesirable side effects:

Unbalanced nutrition. One soft drink contains 120 to 180 calories due to sugar; at the same time, it contains no nutrients.The extra calories of soft drinks will be deposited as fat, which will soon become noticeable.

Fluctuations in blood sugar levels. Because sugar calories are devoid of fibre, they enter the bloodstream quickly, contributing to a temporary energy rush. The body sends a batch of insulin to bring blood sugar levels down to normal levels; this also causes a drop in energy. This sequence of events causes a person to reach again and again for another soft drink or some kind of sweet to keep their energy up.

Disturbance of digestion. When a sugar-containing drink enters the digesting stomach, digestion should slow down or stop altogether until the newly arrived calories have been absorbed.If you only occasionally have a soft drink, it will not make much difference. But if it happens several times a day, digestion slows down and the stomach becomes stressed.

Tooth decay. Studies have convincingly shown that children who drink sugary drinks develop more cavities in their teeth compared to those who do not drink them. The same applies to fruit juices. Based on this, it is better not to drink sugary drinks and juices for a "snack". If you like such drinks, save them for the next meal [2, 3, 4].

Annex 16

Interesting information from the Academy of Health book "To drink or not to drink"

- In many states (in the US) traffic police always have 2 bottles of Coke in their patrol car to wash blood off the highway after an accident.
- To clean the toilet, pour a can of Coke down the sink and... don't rinse for an hour. The citric acid in Coke will remove stains from earthenware.
- To remove rust stains from the car's chrome bumper, rub the bumper with a crumpled sheet of aluminium foil dipped in Kohl's.

- To remove corrosion from car batteries, pour a can of Coke over the batteries and the corrosion will disappear.
- To unscrew a rusted bolt, moisten a Coke cloth and wrap it around the bolt for a few minutes.
- To clean clothes from stains, pour a can of Coke over a pile of dirty clothes, add detergent and machine wash as usual. Coke will help get rid of stains. It will also clean the car windows from road dust.
- The active ingredient in Cola is phosphoric acid. It can dissolve nails in four days.
- For transporting Kola concentrate, the truck must be equipped with special pallets designed for highly corrosive materials.
- Coke distributors have been using it to clean the engines of their trucks for 20 years.
- The only harmless ingredient in sodas is water. Dead, lifeless, distilled, so that its natural taste does not impair the taste of the drink, so that the lemonade produced anywhere in the world meets a strict standard [19].

All non-alcoholic drinks, depending on the composition and preparation method

иоможноподразделитьнагруппы (рис.1).

Рис. 1. Классификация безалкогольных напитков

Annex 17
Characteristics of the current range and classification of soft drinks

The range and quality of non-alcoholic beverages has changed significantly in recent years. In accordance with STB 539-2006 "Soft drinks. General Technical Conditions" the drinks are classified according to five characteristics: carbon dioxide saturation, mass fraction of solids, appearance, processing method, and raw materials used.

Depending on carbon dioxide saturation, two types of drinks are made: carbonated and non-carbonated.

Depending on the mass fraction of solids, beverages can be made non-concentrated or concentrated. Drinks with a mass fraction of solids of 15 % or more are classified as concentrated drinks [11, 12].

Depending on their appearance, beverages can be either clear or cloudy.

Depending on the processing method, drinks are made:

- unpasteurised,
- pasteurised,
- The use of a preservative,
- without the use of a preservative.

Figure 2. Classification of modern functional drinks

Depending on the raw materials used and the manufacturing process, beverages are divided into groups:

- **juice-containing drinks** - drinks made with the addition of natural, alcoholic, concentrated juice or juice base (base) and other components, except artificial sweeteners, artificial flavouring agents and artificial colouring agents. The content of juice in the finished drink should be at least 5 % of the total volume (in terms of natural juice).

- **morses** - drinks made with the addition of juice and other components, except for artificial sweeteners, artificial flavourings and artificial colourings. The content of juice in a ready drink should be not less than 10 % of the total volume, including juice of the same name with the beverage - not less than 5 % (in terms of natural juice). Morsels of lingonberries, cranberries, etc. are known;
- **beverages on herbal raw materials** - beverages made on the basis of extracts or infusions of herbal raw materials (plants, fruits, seeds, etc.) or concentrated bases, which include extracts or infusions of herbal raw materials. Sugars (sweeteners), colouring agents and flavourings shall not be used.
- **Sugary (sweetener) beverages -** beverages made with sweeteners (sugar substitutes).
- **flavoured drinks** - drinks made from natural and identical natural flavourings, essences, essential oils, etc., with the addition of various components.
- **mineral water-based drinks** - drinks made from mineral water with the addition of various components;
- **Special purpose drinks** - drinks for people with diabetes and other conditions.
- **energy drinks -** drinks with a mass fraction of solids of 12% or more, made with the addition of micronutrients with a tonic effect, as well as vitamins,

mineral elements (microelements), etc.

- **vitaminised drinks** - drinks made with a vitamin content of at least 5 % of the daily requirement in 100 g (cm3) of the drink.
- **fermented kvasses** - drinks made by fermentation of grain, vegetable, fruit, berry and other vegetable raw materials. No sweeteners (sweeteners, etc.), colouring agents or flavourings may be used.
- **Kvass beverages** - beverages made on the basis of kvass wort concentrate, grain raw materials with addition of various components. The content of kvass wort concentrate or extract of grain raw material should be not less than 2% of the total volume. Artificial sweeteners, artificial flavourings and artificial colourings shall not be used.

Annex 18

Types of sweet fizzy drinks

Carbonated soft drinks include carbonated water with added syrups. The basis of carbonated drinks is carbonated drinking water. The variety of carbonated drinks is determined by the types of auxiliary raw materials, which include fruit juices, syrups and extracts, sugar, sorbitol, morses, grape wine, tinctures, flavourings, food acids, colouring agents (tints), etc.

Bottled carbonated soft drinks can be divided into five groups:

- ***beverages made from natural raw materials.***

This type includes carbonated drinks based on juices, syrups, extracts and tinctures. They have a significant sugar content (10-12%). They are produced: cherry, pear, cranberry, strawberry drinks, "Lemonade", "Crème Soda" and others.

- ***drinks with synthetic flavourings.***

In organoleptic terms, these drinks must resemble the corresponding fruit and berry raw material. The labels on the bottles of these beverages always indicate the type of food additive introduced into the bottle.

- ***tonic drinks.***

They contain tonic infusions and extracts, so that these drinks can relieve fatigue and have a thirst-quenching effect. The Baikal drink, for example, contains extracts of eucalyptus, laurel and some other plants. The Cola drink series is also referred to as a tonic. Their composition includes infusion of cola nuts rich in caffeine. This drink is only suitable for diabetics, but for the rest of the population it is strictly prohibited, as it interferes with the gastrointestinal tract.

- ***vitaminised drinks.***

They are characterised by an increased content of vitamin C, either in the form of ascorbic acid or as part of highly vitamin-rich extracts of juices and infusions (lemon, orange, blackcurrant).

- ***drinks for diabetics.***

Instead of sugar, the drinks contain sorbitol and other sweeteners. Lemon and orange tinctures and flavourings are used for flavouring. The range includes Pepsi Light, orange, cherry, lemon and citrus drinks [16].

Annex 19 on
certain compounds of gassed beverages

Aspartame E951

A significant advantage of aspartame is that it does not stimulate the development of tooth decay.

Given that aspartame contains residues of the amino acid phenylalanine, it is contraindicated in patients with phenylketonuria. There is evidence that aspartame has been detrimental to human and animal health after long-term use. Tumours have been found in the brains of animals when using this sweetener. In an official statement on December 29, 1996, the U.S. national program "60 Minutes" acknowledged that the testing centres that order aspartame manufacturers were silent about this fact in their reports. There is a very interesting fact that the safety of aspartame was studied by 170 researchers. In 70 experiments commissioned by aspartame manufacturers, it was noted that aspartame was not harmful to humans. Their opinion was joined by seven more independent experts. At the same time, 83 independent institutes and testing centres obtained results that proved aspartame's negative effects on the human body. It has been determined that the use of aspartame can cause headaches, migraines, tinnitus, skin rashes, depression, insomnia and poor coordination.It is currently not officially recommended in the EU for children, and is completely banned for use in baby food under 4 years of age.

The phenylalanine in aspartame changes the sensory threshold and depletes serotonin, which contributes to manic depression, panic attacks, anger and violence when consumed in high doses. Foods containing aspartame are contraindicated in people suffering from phenylketonuria. In the majority of cases (classical form) the disease is associated with a severe reduction or complete absence of the hepatic enzyme phenylalanine-4-hydroxylase, which normally catalyzes the conversion of phenylalanine to tyrosine. As a consequence of the metabolic blockage, side pathways of phenylalanine metabolism are activated and the body accumulates its toxic derivatives - phenylpyruvic and phenyl-lactic acids - which are not formed in the normal way. When heated to +30°C, aspartame decomposes to form the carcinogen formaldehyde and the highly toxic methanol. Ingested methanol (methyl or wood alcohol, which has killed or blinded thousands of alcohol drinkers) is converted to formaldehyde, then to formic acid (the poison of red ants). Formaldehyde is a pungent smelling substance, a Class A carcinogen. So formaldehyde is classified in the same group of substances as arsenic and hydrocyanic acid - deadly poisons!

Drinking drinks containing aspartame does not quench thirst. Saliva is poor at removing residual sweetener from the oral mucosa, leaving an unpleasant feeling in the mouth after drinking a drink containing aspartame

The result is that aspartame drinks become a thirst-quencher rather than a thirst-quencher. As a result, drinks containing aspartame become a thirst-quencher rather than a thirst-quencher. It is therefore necessary to drink Coke with plain water to relieve the feeling of thirst. In addition, the almost completely absent in the normal diet - phenylethylamine and orthophenylacetate - are also formed, an excess of which causes a disturbance of lipid metabolism in the brain. This leads to a progressive decline in intelligence in these patients up to idiocy. However, this can be avoided if the intake of phenylalanine with food is restricted from birth to puberty. Late initiation of treatment has some effect but does not eliminate the irreversible changes in brain tissue that have already occurred. Most modern carbonated drinks contain phenylalanine and warn about it on the label.

Sodium benzoate E211

Sodium benzoate or *C6H5COONa* (E211) is a cough medicine (expectorant). It is used as a preservative. Approved in Russia and European countries. It is used for preserving meat and fish products, margarine, mayonnaise, ketchup, fruit and berry products, drinks. Concentration not more than 150 mg/l. It has strong inhibitory effect on yeasts and moulds including aflatoxinforming fungi, inhibits activity of enzymes responsible for redox reactions in microbial cells as well as enzymes cleaving fats and starch. Products containing sodium and calcium benzoates are not recommended for asthmatics and people who are sensitive to aspirin. Reacts with vitamin C, resulting in benzene (a strong carcinogen).

Orthophosphoric acid (E338)

Orthophosphoric acid (E338), chemical formula: *H3PO4*. Food grade phosphoric acid is used in the production of carbonated water. Its pH (hydrogen index) is 2.8 (highly acidic).

Phosphoric acids are compounds of phosphorus in the +5 degree of oxidation of the general formula *P2O5'nH2O:* orthophosphoric acid - *H3PO4.* From orthophosphoric acid water evaporates easily and it becomes concentrated. Orthophosphoric acid is used for production of fertilizers, in food, textile industry; phosphates are used as phosphoric fertilizers, in enamel and glass production. Orthophosphoric acid is superior to sulphuric acid in its hole-forming activity.

Acesulfame-K (E950)

Safety studies have shown that Sunet is eliminated from the human body unchanged, i.e. it is not digested by the body. It is not broken down, it is not converted into other substances, it has no physiological energy, i.e. it is completely 'calorie-free'. It has no negative impact on the health of diabetics, so it can be used in the production of diabetic confectionery products and food concentrates.

The Joint Expert Committee on Food Additives of the World Food Organisation and the WHO have, after a large number of studies, recognised that Acesulfame-K is approved for use in food and have defined a daily intake of 0-9 mg per 1 kg of body weight.

Sunet is not utilised by oral bacteria, so it does not contribute to tooth decay.

There are a lot of foreign food products in Russia now. And they don't bring the best to us. And it is often difficult for our customers to understand the quality of the product. One of the indicators of quality and safety for consumption is what food additives are contained in this or that product. After all, to give a product these or those qualities it is added a variety of substances, which are sometimes poisonous to the body. Some manufacturers warn the consumer about these additives by listing them in the ingredients using an INS (International Number System) code - a three- or four-digit code preceded by the letter E in Europe.

The letter 'E' stands for Europe and the numerical code is a characteristic of the food additive in the product.

A code number starting with 1 indicates colouring agents, 2 indicates preservatives, 3 indicates antioxidants (they prevent the deterioration of the product), 4 indicates stabilizers (they preserve the consistency of the product), 5 indicates emulsifiers (they maintain the structure), 6 indicates flavour enhancers, 9 indicates anti-foaming agents. Indexes with four digits indicate the presence of sweeteners - substances preserving the crumbliness of sugar or salt, glazing agents.

The use of supplements is legal in many countries and most have no side effects. But doctors have a different opinion.

For example, preservatives E-230, E-231 and E-232 are used in fruit processing (that is where oranges or bananas on shop shelves are from, not spoiling for years!), and they are nothing but phenol, which, getting into our bodies in small doses, provokes cancer, and in large - it is just pure poison. Of course, it is applied in good faith: to prevent spoilage, only on the skin of the fruit.

In addition, there are food additives that are categorically forbidden such as: E-121, a colouring agent (citrus red), and E-240, dangerous formaldehyde. Powdered aluminium is encoded under E-173, which is used to decorate imported sweets and other confectionery products and which is also banned in our country.

But there are some harmless and even useful E's. For example, the additive E-163 (colourant) is just anthocyanin from grape skins. E-338 (antioxidant) and E-450 (stabiliser) are harmless phosphates which are essential for our bones.

Natural dye E-120 (carmine) is produced from scabies, insects that parasitise houseplants. It is used to add colour to jams.

The doctors insist on this conclusion: even those food additives which are made from natural raw materials are still heavily chemically processed. The consequences can therefore be controversial [18].

Classification of food additives:

E100 - E182 colourants
E200 - E280 preservatives
E300 - E391 antioxidants, acidity regulators
E400 - E481 stabilisers, emulsifiers, thickeners
E500 - E585 are different
E600 - E637 flavour enhancers

E700 - E899 spare numbers
E900 - E967 defoamers, glazers, flour improvers, sweeteners
E1100 - E1105 enzyme preparations

Food additives banned:E121, E123, E240.

Food additives **not approved** for use:
E103, E107, E125, E127, E128, E140, E153-155, E160d, E160f, E166, E173-175, E180, E182, E209, E213-219, E225-228, E230-233, E237, E238, E241, E252, E253, E264, E281-283, E302 E303, E305, E308-314, E317, E318, E323-325, E328, E329, E343-345, E349, E350-352, E355-357, E359, E365-368, E370, E375, E381, E384, E387-390, E399, E403, E408, E418, E419 E429-436, E441-444, E446, E462, E463, E465, E467, E474, E476-480, E482-489, E491-496, E505, E512, E519- 523, E535, E537, E538, E541, E542, E550, E552, E554-557, E559, E560 E574, E576, E577, E579, E580, E622-625, E628, E629, E632-635, E640, E641, E906, E908-911, E913, E916-919, E922-926, E929, E942-946, E957, E959, E1000, E1001, E1105, E1503, E1521

Some characteristics of other food additives:

- Hazardous - E110, E123, E127, E129, E150, E151, E173-175, E210, E212, E216-219, E227, E228, E235, E242, E339-341, E400-403, E450-452, E521-523, E541-556, E559, E574-579, E620-625, E900, E912, E951, E954, E965, E967, E999, E1200-1202
- questionable - E102, E104, E120, E122, E124, E141, E150, E161, E173, E180, E241
- carcinogens -E131, E142, E210-217, E239, E330
- destroy vitamin B12 - E220
- disturb the gastrointestinal tract - E221 -226
- impair skin function - E230, E231, E233
- cause a rash - E311, E312
- contain a lot of cholesterol - E320, E321
- disturb digestion - E338, E340, E341, E407, E450, E461-463, E466, E468 [10].

Zeitfracht Medien GmbH
Ferdinand-Jühlke-Straße 7,
99095 - DE, Erfurt
produktsicherheit@zeitfracht.de

FSC
www.fsc.org
MIX
Papier | Fördert
gute Waldnutzung
FSC® C083411

Druck:
CPI Druckdienstleistungen GmbH
im Auftrag der
Zeitfracht Medien GmbH
Ein Unternehmen der Zeitfracht - Gruppe
Ferdinand-Jühlke-Str. 7
99095 Erfurt